MUSEUM

of the

AMERICAN

QUILTER'S

SOCIETY

Additional copies of this book may be ordered from:

American Quilter's Society
P.O. Box 3290
Paducah, KY 42002-3290

@$9.95. Add $1.00 for postage & handling.

Copyright: American Quilter's Society, 1991

This book or any part thereof may not be
reproduced without the written consent of the Publisher.

QUILTS

The Permanent Collection – MAQS

91 quilts

purchased/acquired

during the years 1984

through 1990

American Quilter's Society
P. O. Box 3290 • Paducah, KY 42002-3290

INTROD

In the early 1980's, Bill and Meredith Schroeder were introduced to the world of quilts, and by 1984 they had begun to build an organization dedicated to promoting the accomplishments of today's quilters. The result was the American Quilter's Society (AQS), an organization with thousands of members worldwide. As AQS activities led the Schroeders to some of today's finest quilts, they quickly realized the need for a permanent collection. Thus began the AQS Collection. From 1984 through 1990, a total of 91 quilts were acquired, some purchased, some through Purchase Awards and others by donation.

In 1991, the long-dreamed-of permanent home for that collection became a reality. The Museum of the American Quilter's Society (MAQS), a specially designed 30,000 square foot facility, opened April 25, 1991, in Paducah, KY, to house this collection, exhibits of other quilts, and a range of activities. In or-

UCTION

der to feature a great variety of quilts and quiltmakers, MAQS will not always display the entire permanent collection. For those who wish to see the collection in its entirety – to be able to enjoy each quilt for years to come, AQS is proud to present this new publication, which features a full-color photograph of each of the 91 quilts currently composing the MAQS permanent collection, along with a comment from the maker and her photograph.

Though much of the scope of today's quiltmaking is represented in the MAQS Collection, development of the collection will be ongoing. The current MAQS Collection and this publication are offered as a beginning, the first chapters in a developing documentation of today's quiltmaking. The Schroeders and the Museum of the American Quilter's Society look forward to additions to the collection and future catalogs sharing with others this growing account of the work of today's quiltmakers.

6

Ann Orr's "Ye Olde Sampler"

Ethel Hickman

I made two applique quilt tops before my marriage in 1936, but lost interest in quilts until 1972, when my interest was renewed. Since then I have spent many hours of pleasure making stitches on twenty-six quilts, and received more than my share of honors. This quilt has been my most successful. The flower cluster design is an adaptation of Ann Orr's "Ye Olde Sampler" quilt. The pastel colors and design elements are planned to enhance each other's effectiveness, and the quilting designs to add further to the gracefulness of the applique motifs.

80" x 100", Camden, AR, 1985; poly/cotton blend, cottons; hand appliqued, hand quilted, corded edge.

Autumn Radiance

I tried to express my love of nature in this quilt. The rhythm of the seasons, the vibrant glow of autumn and its colors, the beauty of the dancing patterns of flow and change all fascinate me. This quilt also marks the time when I took all that I had learned in my first three or four years of quilting and made it my own. Studying techniques and designs and practicing on my first projects brought me to the point of wanting to go on my own, to design my quilt, to do my best work and make the quilt that only I could make. I put myself into my work and made what pleased me.

81" x 93", Woodridge, IL, 1986; cottons & cotton blends; hand appliqued, machine pieced & hand quilted; Best of Show Award – 1987 AQS Show.

Sharon Rauba

Basket Of Flowers

Marzenna J. Krol

This pattern, my first original applique design, was inspired by dried flower arrangements I used to make. I had great fun working on this quilt – the pattern developed as the work proceeded. I designed a lot of small flowers and leaves to be appliqued, but used only about a third of them. Making the top was like arranging a dried flower bouquet – choosing the right color, size, shape of flowers and leaves to achieve this "perfect" combination.

72" x 82", Carmel Valley, CA, 1982; cotton/polyesters; hand appliqued & hand quilted. Photo of Marzenna Krol ©1990, T. Krol.

BASKETS I

"Baskets I" continues to be one of my favorite quilts. It reminds me of how much quilting has changed for me since it was made in 1983. Quilting has taken over! I love the excitement, curiosity, gratification and frustrations that are part of the process of creating a quilt. The great opportunity quilting offers me is the constant challenge of the next quilt, inspired by lots of wonderful fabrics.

80" x 96", Brooklyn Park, MN, 1983; cottons; machine pieced, hand appliqued & hand quilted.

Wendy M. Richardson

Bed Of Peonies

Karin Matthiesen

Inspired by a quilt pattern I saw in a magazine, I began quilting in 1971 at the age of 18. My strong point in quilting is workmanship, and I'm more comfortable adapting existing patterns than I am creating original designs. My "Bed of Peonies" quilt was made for the 1986 Mountain Mist contest. I began it in early September of 1985 and finished it the day I had to mail it to the contest, one year later.

85" x 96", Madison, WI, 1986; cottons; hand appliqued & hand quilted; First Place Award, Traditional Pieced, Professional & Gingher Workmanship Award – 1986 AQS Show.

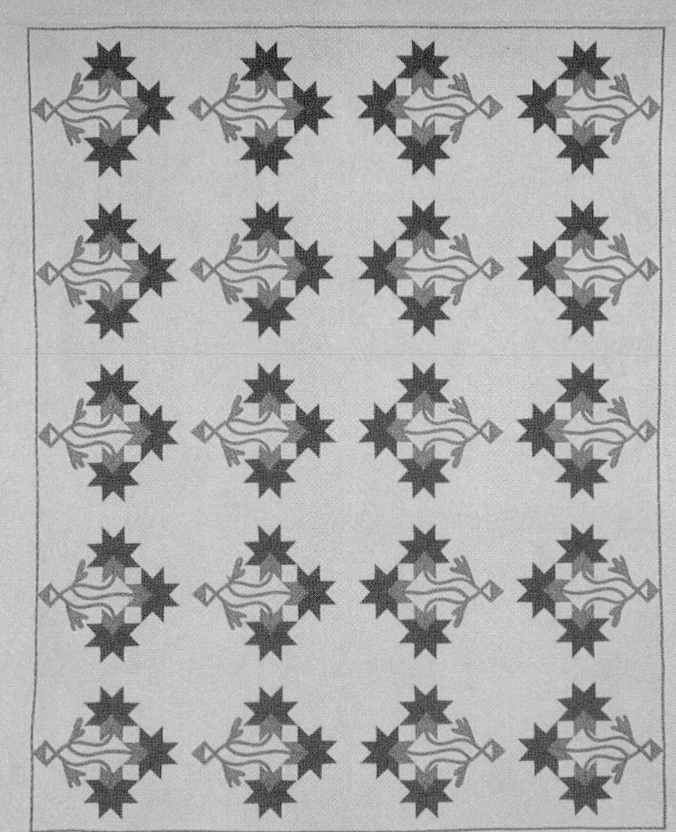

The Beginnings

My first machine quilt was a broken star quilt and my first applique quilt, made for the Statue of Liberty contest, began with an eagle. This quilt combines those images in a tribute to my start as a quiltmaker and to all beginnings. The title came easy – I had a real sense of what it was I wanted to do with this quilt. I am pleased with the results, even though I was working under a tight deadline so some changes had to be made and some short cuts taken.

64" x 84", Rapid City, SD, 1990; cottons, most hand dyed; hand appliqued & hand quilted; Best of Show Award – 1990 AQS Show.

Dawn E. Amos

The Blade

Doreen Speckmann

I guess I am attracted to quilt designs and tend to describe the ones I make in terms of their design instead of the colors. It fascinated me to see what happened when I laid a Swamp Patch block over a Peaky and Spike With Ice Cream Cones block to create the Wingra Star block used in this quilt. I loved the block, but the first two pieces made using it were flops. "The Blade" was my fourth quilt made with this block. For color, I wanted to see the affect of background value changes. I would like people to know that I have never been comfortable with the solid colors. They have always seemed cold and hard. I much prefer working with prints now.

62" x 84", Madison, WI, 1985; cottons; hand pieced & hand quilted, First Place Award, Patchwork, Professional – 1985 AQS Show.

Blazing Splendor

My first quilt was a high school graduation gift for my daughter in 1976 – it depicted the campus of Valparaiso University where she would attend college. A second quilt was not done until 1980. I dabbled in a variety of arts and crafts before determining quilting was my true love. Applique has since become my specialty. I enjoy designing my own work so applique is a natural way to express my ideas. "Blazing Splendor," an original design, is a bright splash of color depicting the Christmas poinsettia. Four shades of red are used for the bracts of the poinsettia and four shades of green for the leaves. The small flowers of yellow-green are embroidered.

38" x 60", LaPorte, IN, 1986; cotton blends; hand appliqued.

Marlene Brown Woodfield

Buffalo Magic

Barbara Pettinga Moore

"Buffalo Magic," my first quilt, is an integration of two long-term interests; buffalo and needlework. The quilt idea evolved and materialized slowly during five summer seasons of employment as a ranger at Badlands National Park in South Dakota. Several of the Plains Indian designs used were sketched from artifacts on exhibit in museums I visited during spring and fall journeys from my home in Shelburne, Vermont, to the Badlands and back.

75" x 90", Shelburne, VT, 1984; cotton broadcloth & suede cloth; hand appliqued & hand quilted; First Quilt Award – 1986 AQS Show.

CITYSCAPE

This "cityscape" quilt was inspired by sketches I did of the Toronto skyline from the 7th floor of the Westbury Hotel. I have always liked the geometry of groups of buildings. All of my wall quilts are a result of drawings done in my yard or while traveling. My husband teaches at St. Lawrence University and we travel a great deal. This quilt is one of a series of cityscapes that are now all in various corporate and private collections.

50" x 64", Canton, NY, 1984; cottons, cotton blends & metallic fabrics; hand sewn; First Place Award, Wall Quilt, Professional – 1985 AQS Show.

Lucretia Romey

16

Clamshell

Arlene Statz

I am a farmer's wife and don't find time for quilting during the summer months. However, from September to April I spend at least four hours a day working on quilts and quilt-related items. I have five grown children and they reap the harvest from my quilt hobby. I am not an artist, so I stick to the more traditional patterns. I wanted to do something in applique so I chose the clamshell used in this quilt. I drew up my own clamshell pattern, much smaller than the ones I found in quilt books, and decided to applique the clamshells onto strips of fabric rather than using them in a block design.

84" x 104", Sun Prairie, WI, 1984; cottons; hand appliqued and hand quilted; Second Place Award, Applique, Amateur – 1985 AQS Show.

Colonial Lady

On November 9, 1909, identical twin girls were born on the Becker farm in northeast Kansas, and I was one of those twins. On the farm, quilting was one of the many "chores," and at an early age our mother had us cut cloth scraps into Nine-Patch, Double Wedding Ring, Log Cabin, and Flower Garden patches – placing them in shoeboxes. No matter the color or patterning, when a box became full, a quilt would be put together by hand or by treadle sewing machine. Quilting was work to us then, so we thought, but now it is my recreation and pleasure, as well as my twin sister's. It is always a pleasure to create something beautiful.

87" x 102", Bremerton, WA, 1984; cottons & cotton blends; hand pieced & appliqued, embroidered & hand quilted.

Louise Stafford

Community Barn Raising

Julee Prose

Mostly self-taught, I have been quilting for about 14 years. My first quilt was a six-point (instead of eight-point) Lone Star because I drafted the pattern wrong. I have learned much about drafting since. "Community Barn Raising" was made specially for the 1987 AQS Show's theme category: Log Cabin. The Log Cabin blocks are set together in the Barn Raising fashion, tying in the Amish theme. Buggies are appliqued around the borders, as if they were going to a barn raising. Small silhouettes of farms are placed throughout the hills.

78" x 102", Ottumwa, IA, 1987; cottons; hand appliqued, machine pieced & hand quilted; First Place Award, Theme (Log Cabin) – 1987 AQS Show.

Corona II: Solar Eclipse

This was my second quilt portraying the solar eclipse. The corona is the envelope of ionized gasses surrounding the chromasphere of the sun, which is visible during a solar eclipse. Both the front and back of the quilt were constructed using a string-piecing technique in which strips of fabric are sewn directly to a full-size drawing of the finished design. The top and back were machine quilted together in a design that spirals out from the center of the disk of the moon to the edge of the sky and into the successive borders. In all of my work, I attempt to achieve multiple levels of visual activity.

76" x 94", Oswego, IL, 1989; hand-dyed cottons; machine pieced & machine quilted; Best of Show Award – 1989 AQS Show.

Caryl Bryer Fallert

Country Garden

Betty K. Patty

I made my first quilt for a Grange contest in Miami County, Ohio, in celebration of our country's bicentennial. I knew then that I had to make more. Like most grandmothers, my first thought was to make one for each of the grand-children. After I had one for each of them I started on one for each of my sons – and it goes on and on. I can't imagine what life would be like without having a quilt in the making. "Country Garden" is based on a Stearns and Foster pattern. While making it, I never lost that excitement that comes when I start a new pattern.

80" X 96", Bradford, OH, 1985; cottons; machine pieced, hand appliqued & hand quilted (with trapunto).

Crossings

My fascination with quilting began as a child when I used to sleep under a Grandmother's Fan quilt made by my great grandmother. Although I never knew her, she was described to me as a "master" quilter and a woman who bought new fabric to make her quilts – not the usual custom in the days of scrap quilts. Soon after the completion of my first quilt in 1982 I was teaching quilting and designing my own patterns. Although many quilts preceded and followed the making of "Crossings," it was made of the first of the hand-dyed fabrics I now sell to quilters and shops around the world.

64" x 52", Lima, OH, 1984; hand-dyed cottons; machine pieced & hand quilted.

Cynthia Buettner

Distant Closeness

Solveig Ronnquist

I hesitate to explain any of my work as I wish the viewer to enjoy the work as he/she sees it. "Distant Closeness" works on two levels for me. As an exhibition piece, the strong perspective draws the viewer from a distance, then reveals the detail panels upon closer observation. On a more spiritual level, the quilt may be seen as an interpersonal relationship which at first is based on superficial observations; closer examination of individual traits and qualities reveals a much more complex and multifaceted person. Once we take the time to observe, we find a richness of details that changes our original view.

75" x 50", Warwick, RI, ©1986; cottons & satins; machine appliqued, hand appliqued & machine quilted.

Dot's Vintage 1983

I'm building a collection of future heirlooms. I like to search for the old quilting motifs, bring them out of hiding between the pages of a book, and use them on my quilts so that this generation and future generations can see and appreciate the motifs and designs used by our ancestors. As I sit and work, I often wonder how our grandmothers would have liked to have had our beautiful, bright fabrics in their scrapbags. In this quilt, to keep an old custom, a quilted grape was deliberately omitted from one of the bunches in the top right panel and "A bird ate the missing grape" was embroidered on the back of the quilt.

84" x 100", Memphis, TN, 1983; cottons; hand appliqued and hand quilted with stuffed motifs; Gingher Workmanship Award – 1985 AQS Show.

Dorothy Finley

Double Wedding Ring

Claudia Dawson

I became interested in quilting when I was about 13 years old, watching my mother make quilts for our beds. The first quilt I made was a Nine-Patch, which I did by hand. When my sewing skills improved, I started making more and more complicated patterns. Making quilts later became my hobby to fill the time while my husband was working away from home on the railroad. "Double Wedding Ring" is made with scraps I saved from my other quilts. I have never entered a contest; I'm just happy making other people happy by doing what I love to do.

93" x 108", Harveill, MO, 1985; cottons & cotton-polyester blends; machine pieced & hand quilted.

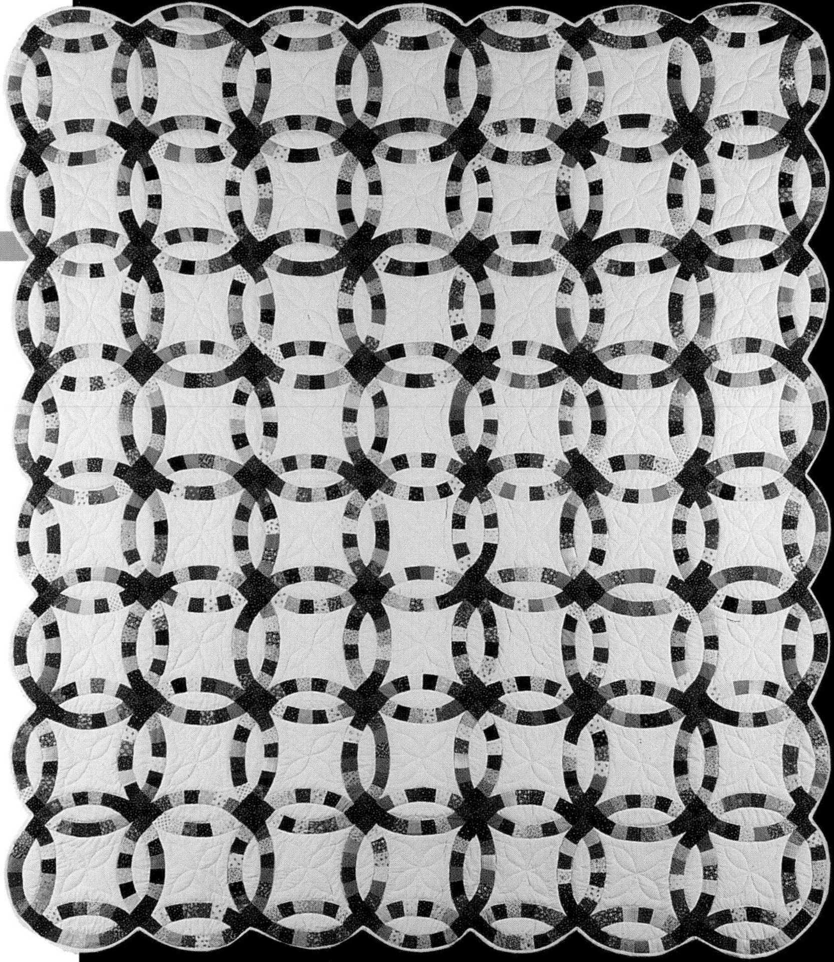

Escape From Circle City

This quilt was created as a catharsis. I was very frustrated over the results of the Great American Quilt Festival I in 1986 and "threw together" this quilt in a few weeks. I used blacks and grays because I was in a "dark" mood. The "escape" was my attempt to break away from traditional into contemporary. It completely absolved all the anger and in fact evoked much humor as people commented on the tongue-in-cheek manner of poking fun at traditional quiltmaking.

76" x 86", Sumter, SC, ©1986; cottons & poly-blends (some fabrics from the 1950's); machine pieced, hand appliqued & hand quilted; First Place Award, Innovative Pieced, Amateur – 1987 AQS Show.

Sylvia Pickell

Feathered Friends

Wilma Johnson

This quilt is a wildlife enthusiast's dream. Displayed are fifteen different species of waterfowl at rest among cattails in rippling water. Each bird was carefully researched and designed as true to nature as possible. We both began sewing in our teenage years. In 1980, after a long fascination with and appreciation of wildlife, the two of us, sisters-in-law, began searching for realistic waterfowl patterns for projects for our homes. When none were found, we tried our hands at designing. The results were rewarding. Our patterns and books have since been shipped to shops and individuals around the world.

63" x 91", Symsonia, KY, 1984; cottons; hand appliqued and hand quilted.

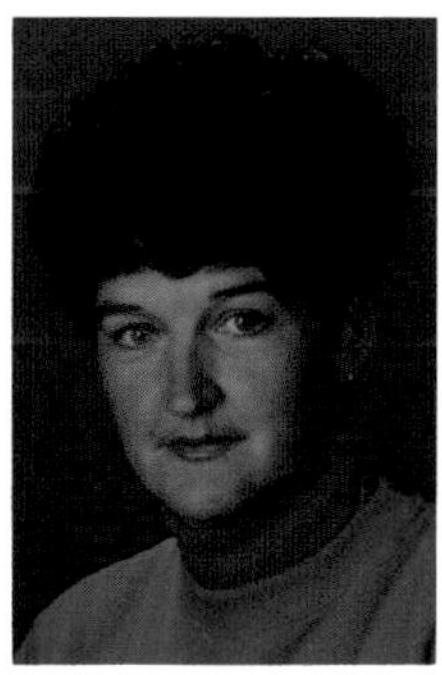

Carolyn Johnson

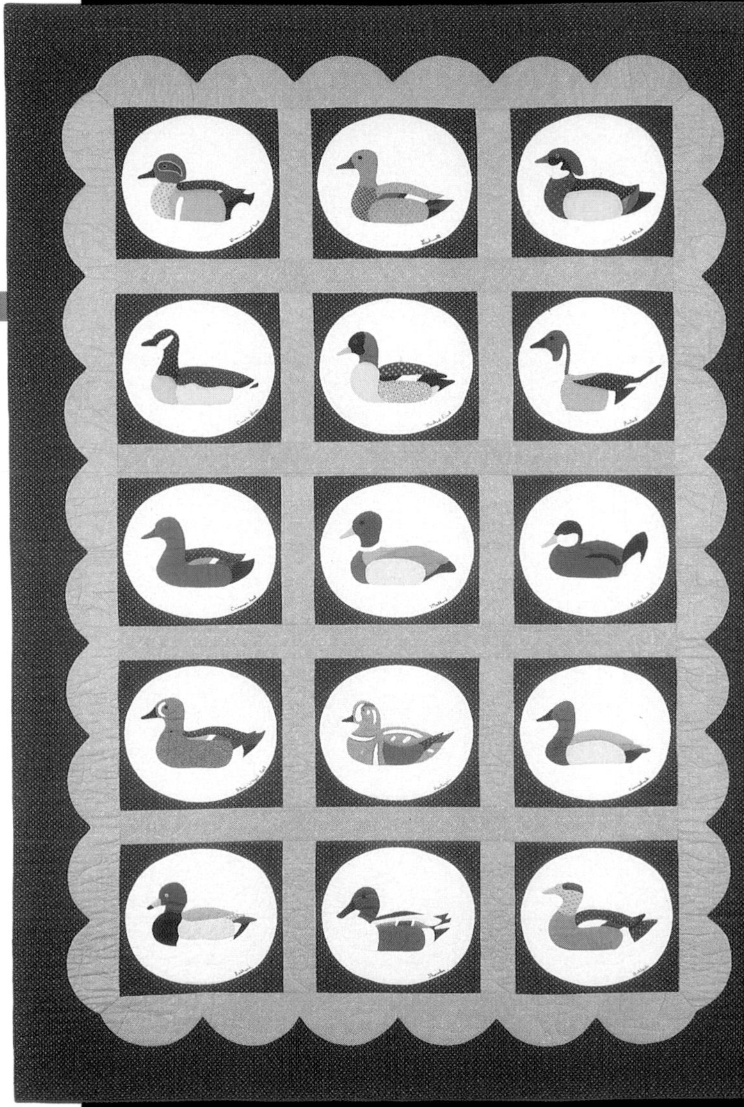

Feathered Star Sampler

My quilting career started as a teenager when my mother insisted that I learn to quilt; I have been very thankful for her getting me started; however, it wasn't until after a back surgery in 1975 that I really became involved with quilting. In order to use up some of Mother's scraps (and keep myself busy) I pieced a Thousand Pyramids; from then on I was hooked! "Feathered Star Sampler" was made for the Indianapolis "Blocks and Stars" contest. My favorite color combinations are navy and beige, so when I saw Jinny Beyer border prints in this combination, it was love at first sight. I was intrigued by the different designs that could be made by cutting up the borders.

110" x 110", Rockville, IN, 1983; cottons; hand pieced and hand quilted; Second Place Award, Patchwork Professional – 1985 AQS Show.

Imogene Gooch

Flower Basket

Cletha Bird

A picture of a very famous and beautiful quilt by Grace Snyder inspired me to make my own Flower Basket quilt. What a challenge for a first quilt – to try to create something that even resembled her would be quite an achievement. Had I known more about the challenges of quiltmaking, I am sure that I would not have tried that particular design! I encountered many problems and almost gave up many times, but my husband and son kept encouraging me to finish it. Now, quilting has become an essential part of my life. I attend many quilt shows in order to be inspired by the beautiful designs and innovative techniques other quilters have used in making beautiful works of art.

95" x 100", Hope, IN, 1986; cottons & cotton blends; machine pieced & hand quilted.

Flower Basket Sampler

In 1982 I decided I should start looking for another interest to occupy some of my time. My youngest boy was in high school so I could see that I would soon face the empty nest syndrome. I had always liked to sew, so when I read about a quilters guild being newly organized at the fabric store in the nearby town of Wahpeton, ND, I decided to give it a try. I went to my first meeting and have been going every month since then.

90" x 112", Mooreton, ND, 1984; cottons & cotton blends; hand and machine pieced, hand quilted and hand embroidered.

Theresa Klosterman

Galaxy of Quilters

Lois K. Ide

This quilt, designed from the traditional Eight-Pointed Star patchwork pattern or Stars and Stripes design, was made to honor quilters and those who contributed to the quilters' world in some significant way during the 1980's. It not only honors those whose signatures appear on the 64 signature stars but there is also a block which states "Salute also the hundreds of fine quilters who have not signed in." In addition, there are 18 "happenings" embroidered in white within the quilted stars in the border. It is the wish of the designer and maker that this quilt will bring many memories to all who view it.

87" x 107", Bucyrus, Ohio, 1983; cottons & cotton blends; hand appliqued, embroidered, machine pieced & hand quilted.

Grandmother's Engagement Ring

I was exposed to quilts for the first time when I met Lucy Happ, a quilter from Oklahoma. I was a doctor and had joined the Navy and Lucy was a career Navy nurse. I admired her quilts, bought some quilt books and taught myself to quilt. Now I make three to four quilts per year and use a large frame that is always set up in the living room. This quilt was fun to make. My husband helped me choose which Mountain Mist pattern to make – one which would be a real show-stopper.

76" x 94", Vicksburg, MS, 1986; cottons; machine pieced & hand quilted; Third Place Award, Traditional Pieced, Amateur – 1986 AQS Show.

Polly M. Sepulvado, MD

Grandmother's Engagement Ring

Arlene Statz

When my youngest daughter was engaged to be married I decided to make this quilt for her. It is a Mountain Mist pattern, a combination of patchwork and applique. I like working with small pieces and this quilt has many. When the American Quilter's Society decided they wanted the quilt for their collection, I decided to part with it. Needless to say, my daughter did get a quilt. I made her a Pineapple Log Cabin. I devote most of my time to quilting. I have five grown children and most of my quilts are passed on to them and the grandchildren.

74" x 96", Sun Prairie, WI, 1986; cottons; machine pieced, hand appliqued & hand quilted.

Gypsy In My Soul

Quilting is what I do! It has everything I like to do in one activity – color selections, designing, sewing, mathematical precision in templates and the quilting stitch as bas relief. It is truly addicting and my obsession. My work begins with the quilt blocks created and named by quilters of the past. This quilt manipulates the traditional Queen Charlotte's Crown block, adds plain blocks and applique and lets color do the rest. If my work looks traditional to some and contemporary to others, I have achieved the blending of old and new which is my goal.

66" x 84", Conshohocken, PA; 1987; cottons & cotton-polyester; hand pieced, hand appliqued & hand quilted; Best of Show Award – 1988 AQS Show.

Jane Blair

Hearts And Stars

Judy (Hendry) Seidel

Craftsmanship is vital to me. My roots are in tradition and I must craft a quilt as carefully as I'm able. I love hand quilting, as it centers me. I feel best when I'm able to quilt a little bit each day. I thrive on tedious hand-work such as stippling, applique, embroidery and beading. Unlike most of my quilts, this quilt was made on a whim for no one in particular. I'd been taking my quilting too seriously. I came up with this design on the belief that some new baby would like to sleep under stars and hearts that were stitched with love and care.

40" x 48", Fort Collins, CO, 1984; cottons & cotton blends; hand & machine pieced, hand appliqued and hand quilted (and stuffed).

INCANTATION

My pieces attempt to communicate a sense of invisible life within seemingly inanimate forms; a hidden current of vitality through the universe with an order and harmony like the "music of the spheres." These somewhat surrealistic structures follow their own natural laws, inhabit their own spaces, and interact serenely beyond our conscious awareness. "Incantation" is influenced by a sense of the manifestation of the spiritual in the physical world. Light streams from an outside source, to be contained, and to inspire, wherever it is willingly received.

29" x 44", 1984, Brooks, ME; cottons; painted silk (fiber-reactive dyes), machine & hand pieced, hand quilted.

Janice Anthony

Lancaster County Rose

Irene Goodrich

My ancestors on both sides of the house were quilters. My mother taught me to sew when I was about four years old and she started me on simple quilt patches which became a top by the time I had started to school. My second top was hand sewn in the summer that I was thirteen, but neither became quilts until I was in my forties. Quilting became a serious business with me in 1967 when I decided to make a quilt for each of my nieces and nephews, brothers and sisters, and parents. By 1990 I had put my fifty-fifth quilt in the frame. I have grown right along with the revival and have come a long way since then.

90" x 110", Columbus, Ohio, 1980; cottons & cotton blends; hand pieced & hand quilted.

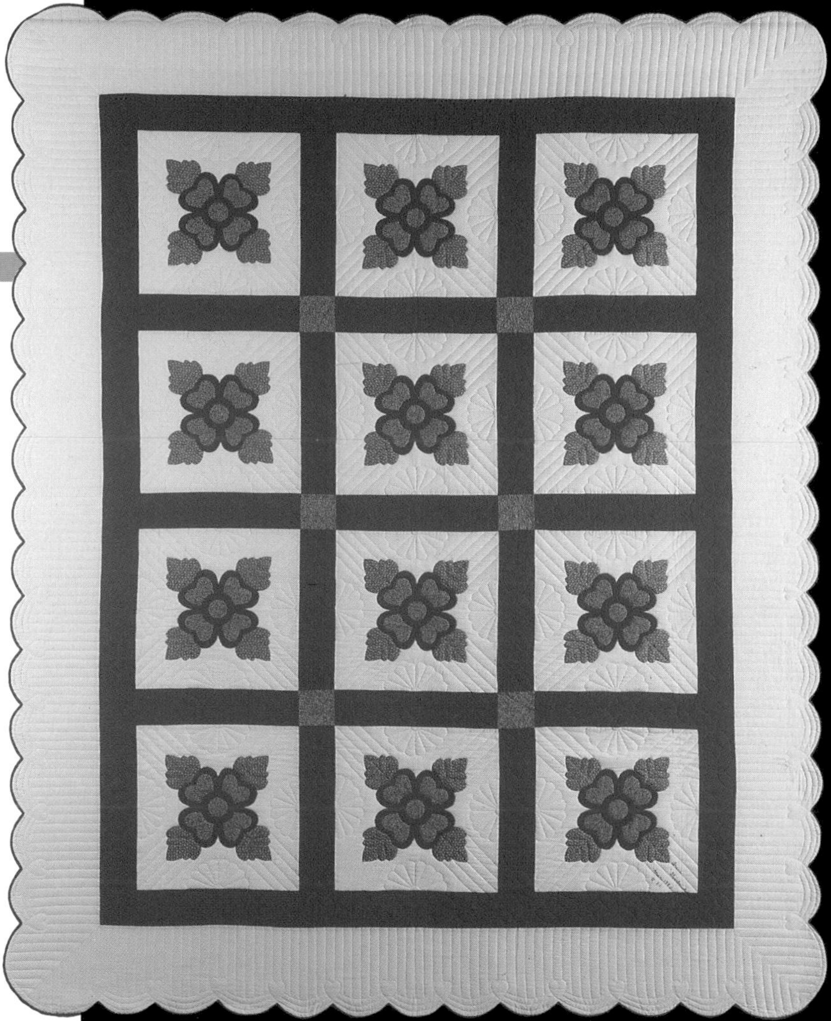

A Little Bit Of Candlewicking

There is something about the understated elegance of an all-white quilt that makes them special. The size of this quilt is unusual because it was made especially to fit an antique spool bed. In keeping with the overall look of the quilt, it was signed and dated in candlewicking knots in the lower center border section of the quilt. I'm particularly interested in those types of quilts that have survived in fewer numbers, such as candlewicked, stenciled and whole-cloth quilts.

64" x 97", Greenwood, IN, 1983; cotton unbleached muslin, cluny lace & satin ribbon; candlewicked, machine pieced & hand quilted; Third Place Award, Other Techniques, Amateur – 1986 AQS Show.

Bonnie K. Browning

Looking Back On Broken Promises

Dawn E. Amos

I'm not very comfortable explaining my work. My quilts mean something to me, but they may mean something very different to someone else and that is all right with me. I don't like to limit people's view of my work. For this quilt I started with one figure – the mountain man or white settler. The rest of the quilt developed from that. I often work that way, placing the first completed figure on my wall, looking at it and then seeing possibilities. The quilts are built up figure by figure.

53" x 38", Rapid City, SD, 1989; cottons, most hand dyed; hand appliqued & hand quilted; Best Wall Quilt – 1989 AQS Show.

MALTESE CROSS

Quilting is exciting because it draws on a long folk tradition, yet leaves unlimited room for innovation. My quilts use the tradition of geometric repeat patterns as a springboard for exploration. This quilt is based on a diagram of the Maltese Cross embroidery stitch, and combines a medallion format with a repeat pattern. In our mechanized economy it's immensely gratifying to be able to spend hundreds of hours constructing one fine object. I am as proud of my dedication and skill in handling fabric as I am of my design sense. I hope to be seen as a part of both the fine art and craft traditions.

88" x 76", Milwaukee, WI, 1987; cottons; hand & machine pieced, hand quilted.

Chris Kleppe

Many Stars

Mary E. Kuebler

As a twelve year old, I made my first quilt, the Dresden Plate. I have no idea where it is or what happened to it. I loved to draw, and would sit on the front steps of our home, and draw on paper bags or wrappings of any kind. In the late fifties, I was able to attend classes in batik with the late Jim Nordmeyer at the Baker-Hunt Foundation in Covington, Kentucky. Batik is an ancient art form and close to my heart. To date I have completed some eighteen quilts, six of which are batik. My quilts are scattered among our children, grandchildren and friends.

77" x 96", Cincinnati, OH, 1984; cottons; batiked & hand quilted.

Maple Leaf

I was born and educated in Warsaw, Poland, and came to this country in 1981. When I was living in Lancaster County, Pennsylvania, and working for the Mennonites, everybody had a quilting frame at home and quilting was a part of a daily routine. The Mennonites' patience, understanding and love for quilting made me understand what quilting is all about. "Maple Leaf" was one of my first quilts. Having lived in Vermont for over one year, I had a chance to see the changing colors of leaves in fall. They left a lasting impression on me. In my top, I tried to imitate the variety of colors I'd seen.

84" x 97", Carmel Valley, CA, 1984; cottons & cotton blends; machine pieced & hand quilted. Photo of Marzenna Kroll ©1990, T. Krol.

Marzenna J. Krol

Mariner's Compass

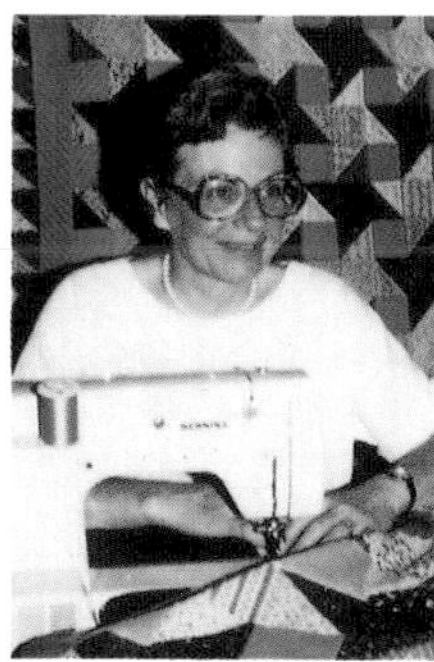

Deborah Warren Techentin

Since early childhood I have been fascinated by making things with needle and thread. For many years this interest was channeled into home sewing and needlework; nothing was bought that could be made. In 1982 I took a quilting class, and I was hooked. This quilt was made in tribute to my father's long-time passion for sailing. It features a Mariner's Compass center on a dark blue ground, surrounded by four Safe Harbor corner blocks and a border of Lost Ships. This is framed by a second Sawtooth edged border, and finally by an outer border repeating the compass theme in more subdued colors.

78" x 90", Kalamazoo, MI, 1985; cottons; machine & hand pieced, hand quilted.

May Shadows

Joyce Murrin comments about her background: "With eyes and ears open, reading then asking plenty of the right questions, I have forged ahead towards being a master craftsman in quiltmaking." Jean Evans adds: "Fortunately, design comes easy so there is security in knowing there is more where that came from, regardless of time, which remains a luxury when dividing my non-teaching hours between quiltmaking, and many other pursuits. And to think there is still time to make quilts such as 'May Shadows' with my identical twin, Joyce Murrin!"

60" x 60", Medina, OH & East Marion, NY, 1985; cottons & blends; hand appliqued & quilted.

Jean Evans and Joyce Murrin

A Midwinter Night's Dream

Nancy Ann Sobel

My mother died when I was three years old, but God gave me a wonderful country grandmother who spent quality time teaching me to use a needle and thread. With her encouragement, patience and enthusiasm, I darned my first sock at the age of four, learned to use her treadle sewing machine at age seven and started my first quilt top when a young teenager. "A Midwinter Night's Dream" is the last in a series of four quilts called "Starring the Seasons," which began in 1984 as a challenge to myself to make a "show" quilt. It was my original design based on the old traditional Crown of Thorns block.

99" x 99", Brooktondale, NY, 1988; cottons; machine pieced, hand appliqued & hand quilted; Gingher Workmanship Award – 1990 AQS Show.

MORISCO

If my work looks traditional to some and contemporary to others, I have achieved the blending of old and new which is my goal. My work begins with the quilt blocks created and named by quilters of the past. This quilt manipulates and uses large, small, rectangular, square and half blocks of the traditional Bleeding Heart design. Color does the rest.

80" x 90", 1984, Conshohocken, PA; cottons & cotton/polyester fabrics; hand pieced & hand quilted.

Jane Blair

Nature's Walk

Hazel B. Reed Ferrell

A native of West Virginia, I grew up in the hills near the Ohio River. I walked three miles through the countryside to attend a one-room school. I cannot remember not being involved in sewing as I was the only girl in a family of four. The basics of sewing and quilting were learned at my mother's and Grandma's knees, and quilts were a necessity as well as a tradition. I have been quilting on my own since 1956. My husband and I live on a farm, and nights I relax with my sewing. The inspiration for the design of "Nature's Walk" was derived from my love of nature and the beautiful flowers.

99" x 103", Middlebourne, WV, 1983; cotton blends; hand appliqued & hand quilted.

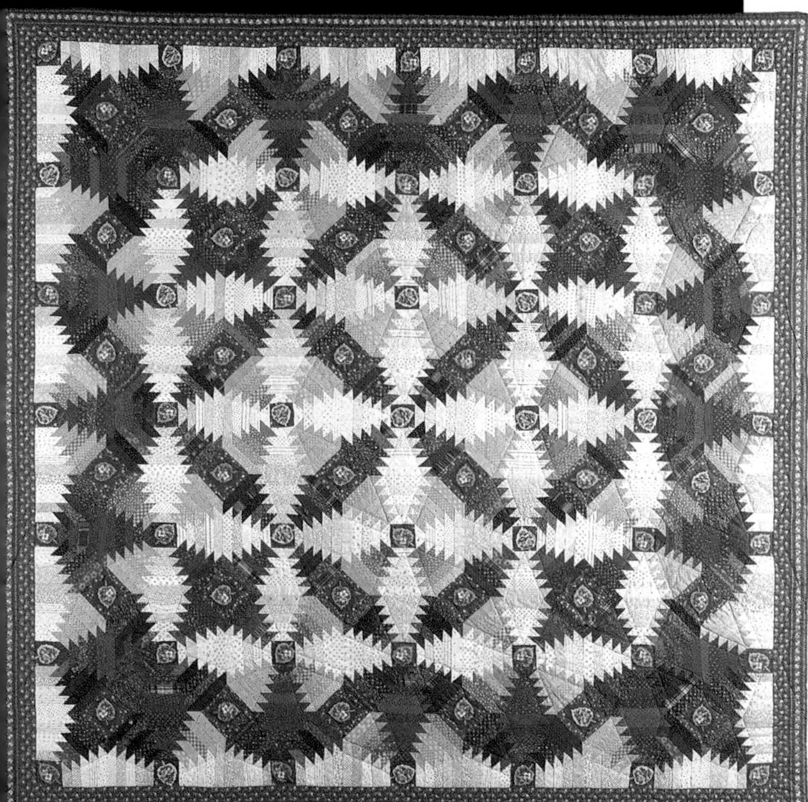

Ne'er Encounter Pain

After teaching several years I had only instructional quilts to my credit. There was no one quilt that was truly my own in thought. The choice of blocks grew from years of working with the Kaleidoscope pattern. Finding that the Kaleidoscope and Pineapple blocks had eight-sidedness in common, I took the design from my first Kaleidoscope quilt effort and applied it to Pineapple piecing. 1980's calicoes were combined with 1880's calicoes in a random placement. Just as the piecing process drew near, my husband was diagnosed as having a brain tumor. I attribute my calmness during this period to the piecing of "Ne'er Encounter Pain," the 154th quilt I have made.

90" x 90", New Hampton, CT, 1983; cottons; hand pieced and hand quilted.

Mary Golden

Neon Nights

Moneca Calvert

I strive for my work to have the technical appearance of wonderful traditional quilts of the past with designs and patterns I hope will become traditional for this era. I have thoroughly explored the traditional clamshell pattern and tried to give it an update through size, piecing and placement. "Neon Nights" is a bordered medallion consisting of large clamshells that have been pieced in several different designs and set in a contemporary placement. I prefer to use fabric that is available to all quilters. I have no desire to dye, paint, stencil or create any surface treatment. I like to make unusual fabrics work for me.

53" x 53", Rocklin, CA, 1986; cottons & cotton blends; machine pieced & hand quilted.

New York Beauty

I make only functional pieces – that is – my quilts are made to be used, loved, enjoyed, shared, washed, and yes, used up, worn out. While I was in Mobile, Alabama, helping document old quilts, I saw many variations of this wonderful old design. I came home knowing that I just had to make this pattern. I wanted my New York Beauty quilt to be oblong, not square, so the circles would be more complete, and set on the diagonal. After trying several patterns I drafted the one I used in order to get the proportions I wanted. I had been saving the red fabric for seven years for some special quilt and this seemed the right one.

77" x 90", Vicksburg, MS, 1986; cottons; hand pieced, machine pieced & hand quilted; First Place Award, Traditional Pieced, Professional – 1987 AQS Show.

Martha B. Skelton

Night And Noon Variation

Joyce Ann Tennery

A needle and thread are familiar tools for me, as I learned sewing skills from my mother. My work in the field of quiltmaking is the process of carrying on the tradition into the 1990's. Exploring design and color are my main goals. "Night and Noon Variation" was designed to explore miniature quilt blocks. A thirteen-inch block was drafted to obtain a six-inch center for the miniatures. There are twelve miniatures, with the two middle squares being the same pattern. The fabric placement disguises the duplication of the pattern in these two squares.

72" x 92", Oak Ridge, TN, 1987; cottons; hand pieced & hand quilted.

NIGHT BLOOM

My work begins with the quilt blocks created and named by quilters of the past. I am interested in innovative design and color, but still want the end result to be more pleasing to the eye than shocking to the soul; somewhere between the faded gems of the past and the vivid harshness of the present. If my work looks traditional to some and contemporary to others, I have achieved the blending of old and new which is my goal. This quilt uses the traditional Basket of Scraps block – one row in one direction, the next row in the opposite direction. Color does the rest.

56" x 72", Conshohocken, PA, 1985; cottons & cotton/polyesters; hand pieced & hand quilted; First Place Award, Wall Quilt, Professional – 1986 AQS Show.

Jane Blair

Nosegay

Judy Simmons

I should have been suspicious – at the mere age of five I was more intrigued with my mother's box of scrap fabrics than anything else. I've been sewing for as long as I can remember. My love for applique surpasses any other technique in quilting. I feel it gives me the greatest freedom of creative expression. The more intricate, the better – I'm a lover of detail. "Nosegay" is my smallest piece. I enjoyed working with a round shape and an uneven edge. It was a challenge. I've always loved broderie perse, so using all cottons, I created this broderie perse piece. I enjoyed appliqueing fine lines, stems, etc. – hence the ribbons surrounding the bouquet.

36" diameter, Coral Springs, FL, 1986; cottons; hand appliqued & hand pieced.

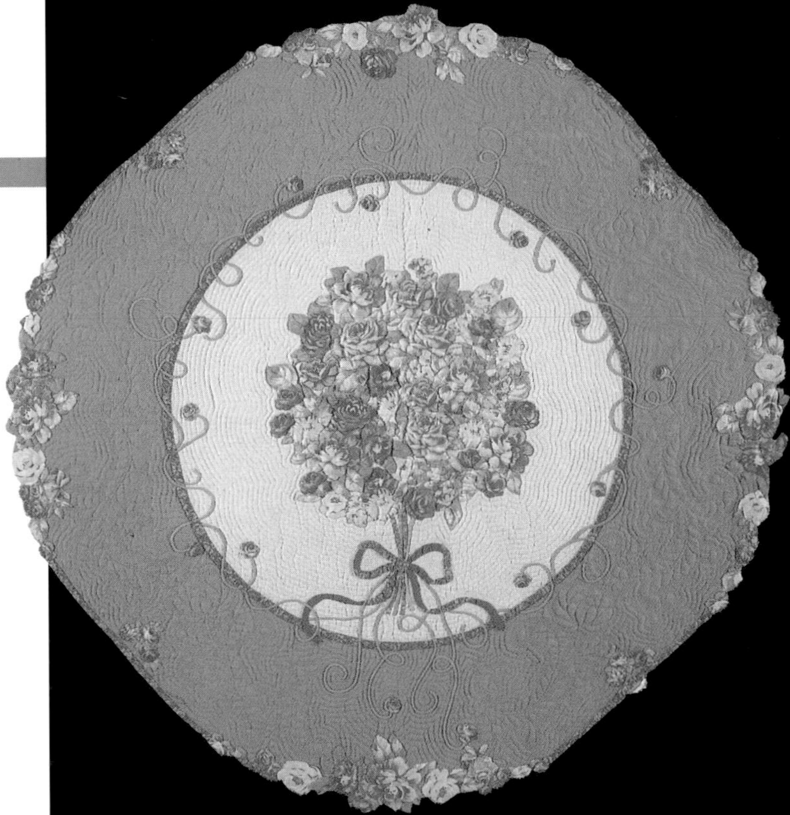

Nothing Gold Can Stay

I have always been interested in the cycles of nature, the way living things change in shape and color, the way living things have different forms at birth, maturity and senescence. The dandelion is a particularly good example. It has the added wonder of sharp, jagged leaves contrasted with its soft button flower. Best of all, its "white hair" drifts away to plant itself later and begin a new cycle. Personally the dandelion is a family symbol. I have always hailed a field of yellow as one of the first joyous bursts of spring. My sons used to bring me handfuls as gifts.

71" x 57", Evanston, IL, 1985; cottons, some hand dyed; hand pieced, machine pieced, hand appliqued, reverse appliqued & hand quilted; First Place Award, Wall Quilt, Professional – 1986 AQS Show.

Marion Huyck

Ohio Bride's Quilt

Debra Wagner

I chose to make this quilt because it contains the elements I find most appealing in quilts. It has a strong graphic design of only two colors, complex triangle piecing and a wonderful quilting design that is heavily trapuntoed. Like many of my quilts it reflects my obsession with mid-nineteenth century textiles. Although the pattern is straight from 1860 the technique is high tech, with the entire quilt being machine made from the piecing and quilting to the trapunto.

To me, combining antique design and modern methods seems like the best of both worlds.

81" x 81", Hutchinson, MN, 1989; cottons; machine pieced & machine quilted, with trapunto; First Place Award, Other Techniques & Viewer's Choice Award, Quilts – 1990 AQS Show.

ORCHARD BEAUTY

"Keep your stitches small and as even as you can." My grandmother's words still echo with the same intensity as they did forty years ago. Quilting is part of my heritage, and as I work over the same quilting frames that she used, I am still impressed by her penchant for neatness. Applique designs are my favorite, and each quilt is completely hand stitched. Patterns that I create are used once, then destroyed to insure that each quilt is one of a kind. I love to paint with needle and thread and I hope people get as much enjoyment out of viewing my work as I have had in creating it.

88" x 105", Guntersville, AL, 1986; Dacron/cotton blends; hand appliqued & hand quilted.

Toni Kron

Oriental Fantasy

Katherine Inman

The Oriental design came as a result of living two years in Southeast Asia. One night was spent with paper and crayons at the kitchen table. By morning the design was finalized down to the last detail. The Chinese symbols quilted in blue were from my imagination and have no meaning that I am aware of. The outside border quilting is bamboo with Chinese temples in each corner. In the center panel is my name in Chinese. My objective was to make a quilt that would have a quiet and peaceful effect in the room. My hope is that this was accomplished.

82" x 98", Athens, OH, 1984; cottons; hand appliqued, hand embroidered & hand quilted; Best of Show Award – 1985 AQS Show.

Oriental Poppy

The oldest of five children, I began sewing at the age of twelve. I began quilting in 1976 during the bicentennial celebration. I now have my own studio where I also teach quilting and design original clothing using quilting, smocking and French hand sewing techniques. Pieced, hand appliqued and hand quilted in black thread on polished cotton, this quilt took eighteen weeks for me to complete, working seven days a week at ten, twelve and fourteen hour sittings each day. Because of the sheen and its hard finish, the material was rather difficult to quilt.

90" x 95", Pasadena, MD, 1986; polished cottons; machine pieced, hand appliqued & hand quilted.

Leureta Beam Thieme

Outlooks

Barbara Lydecker Crane

"Outlooks" was the first in a series of ten window quilts which explored openness and barriers, freedom and restrictions. In this quilt, I especially enjoyed making each window (and keyhole) view different, to create a tantalizing array of glimpsed, idyllic scenes. Into these scenes are sewed tiny objects which seem to "inhabit" their fabric environments. Creating the effect of stonework in the gray fabric was a laborious process of hand quilting and stippling. Stippling was also used to darken the area over the doorway arch. A full-size key for "use" by any viewer who feels hemmed in or imprisoned is also added.

60" x 54", Lexington, MA, 1984; cottons (some hand dyed) & cotton blends; hand pieced, machine pieced & hand quilted; embellished with small objects; Third Place Award, Wall Quilt, Amateur – 1985 AQS Show.

Peace And Love

While making this quilt I called it "My Blue Shadow," but my late husband Dr. Thomas Stone renamed it "Peace and Love." His reasons were the rose depicted a lovely peace rose he had planted in our garden as a gift to me shortly after our marriage. The dove within the heart he said was for our devout and everlasting love for each other. Shortly after the quilt was completed he lost his battle with cancer and never saw it hang in any show. It has won several blue ribbons. I dedicate the quilt to Tommy's memory, with my love.

96" x 92", Mayfield, KY, 1985; cottons, lace & ribbon; hand quilted with embroidery thread.

Frances Stone

Persian Paradise

Jean K. Mathews

I have made wedding quilts, baby quilts, wallhangings, quilted clothing and various items for myself and my family. I still love the traditional patterns and like to experiment with them using unusual colors and settings, but creating something entirely new really excites me. I purchased a handmade Oriental rug in Greece in 1985, and as a result, became inspired to make an applique quilt that looked similar to the unusual shapes and colors in the rug. I drew the main Oriental shapes on large newsprint and then used reverse applique to apply to the background fabric. I then experimented with flowers, leaves and shapes to enhance the different areas.

72½" x 59", Pendleton, IN, 1986; cottons & polyester/cotton chintz; hand appliqued, reverse appliqued & hand quilted.

Phoenix Rising

The Phoenix is a powerful symbol about dying and being reborn out of the ashes of living. I love living in a city whose name reminds me of that ongoing human experience. In making the quilt, I spent a lot of time looking, buying, discarding fabrics, until I had the flow of hue and value that would make the massive wings seem to lift. I found the head to be the hardest; it had to look strong and project the intent to rise up out of the chaos, or despair, or whatever. Later, I noted a picture of myself and dog in front of the quilt, and found that the head was Baron's, the gentle, watchful doberman.

95½" x 80", Phoenix, AZ, 1987; cottons; machine pieced, hand appliqued, hand painted (background fabric) & hand quilted.

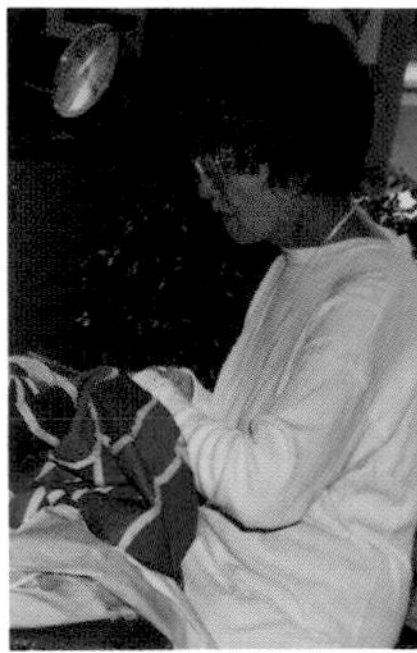

Nancy Clark

Pineapple Log Cabin

Jane Hall

I am a quiltmaker, a teacher, a judge and an appraiser. I am intrigued by the interaction of colors and fabrics and by the graphic designs. I like to use traditional patterns in innovative ways. I love working with quilts and quilters, from almost any angle: it fulfills my creative urges, gives me a satisfying tie to the past and surrounds me with neat people who share my feelings. This is the first large Pineapple quilt I made using a technique I have used and taught successfully for ten years now. I draw the pattern on a foundation (fabric or paper) and placing the fabrics on the un-drawn side of the foundation, stitch from the drawn side, on the lines. This all but guarantees "Perfect Pineapples."

50" x 68", Raleigh, NC, 1985; cottons; machine pieced.

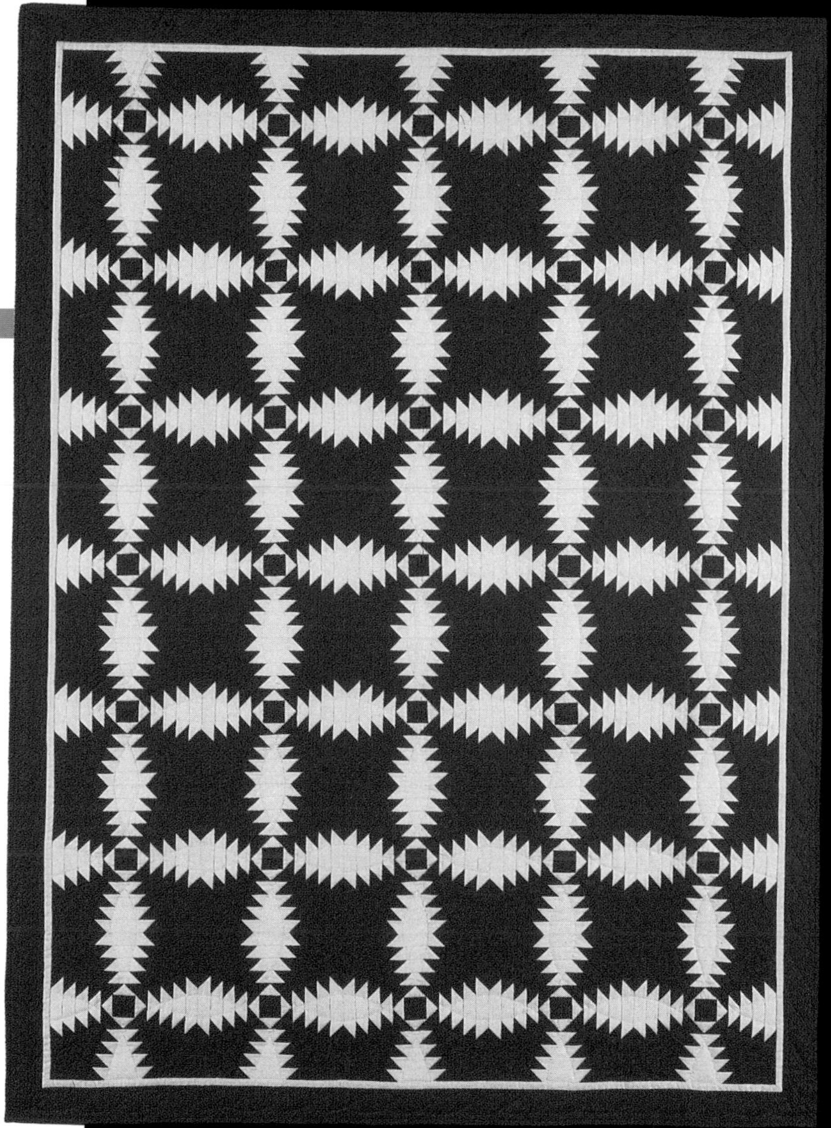

President's Wreath Variation

I began quilting in 1973. I inherited two tops I wanted to finish, joined the National Quilting Association to learn, won a ribbon in my first show and have been making quilts since then. I have won awards in a number of contests and photos of my quilts have appeared in magazines. All of these opportunities have been most satisfying.

"President's Wreath Variation" did not start out as a variation. After cutting, I discovered the pattern was mismarked so I had to make radical changes. I also added sashing and designed an original flower border. The blocks were stipple quilted to add further interest and contrast.

72" x 96", Hyattsville, MD, 1986; cottons & cotton/ polyesters; hand appliqued, machine pieced & hand quilted; Second Place Award. Applique, Amateur – 1986 AQS Show.

Doris Amiss Rabey

PROSPERITY

Elaine M. Seaman

I gave up on calicoes several years ago and eliminated solids (recently) because I thought painters did better with solids than quilters did. Prints – large florals, viney, sinewy organic designs, paisleys, and geometrics – are the true challenge. They are foolers. They look different up close and far away. How they are cut is important. How they are combined is essential. That's why I enjoy using them.

84" x 84", Kalamazoo, MI, 1985; cottons; hand pieced, machine pieced & hand quilted.

Quilted Counterpane

I especially enjoy the actual quilting, rather than the piecing or marking. The quilts I work on become a part of me, making them difficult to part with. I started "Quilted Counterpane" in January 1984 and quilted the finishing stitches in November 1985. The pattern is an adaptation of a Mountain Mist design. I marked the quilt using a homemade light box. I do not use a thimble but still am able to achieve twelve stitches to the inch.

72" x 102", Delmar, NY, 1985; polished cotton; hand quilted; Second Place Award, Other Techniques, Amateur – 1986 AQS Show.

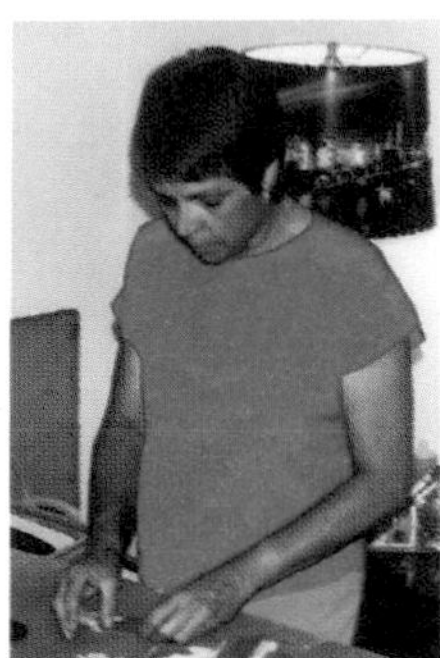

Patricia Spadaro

Reach For The Stars

Jan Lanahan

"Reach for the Stars" is a tribute to the crew of the Challenger. My first instinct as a quilter was to make a quilt for each family member of the Challenger crew (quilts give hugs when you wrap them around you) but realized that was impossible so I decided to make one special quilt as a tribute. I used all types of fabrics from my scrap bag, overdyeing & bleaching to get the desired effect.

66" x 82", Walkersville, MD, 1986; cottons, flannels, satins & other scraps (some over-dyed & bleached); hand pieced & hand quilted; Second Place Award, Innovative Pieced, Amateur – 1987 AQS Show.

Red Poppies

"Red Poppies" has always been one of my favorites. I am no longer working in the style of this quilt, but it is the best of a series of medallion quilts that I worked on from 1982 through 1984. At the time I designed "Red Poppies" I had been experimenting with my kaleidoscope as a means of finding design ideas; the center is a kaleidoscope-type design. I originally designed this quilt for a couple living in an old farm house full of antiques. When it was finished, I thought it looked much too contemporary for a "country" house, so I kept it and made a new quilt for them.

72" x 90", Oswego, IL, 1983; cottons; machine pieced & hand quilted.

Caryl Bryer Fallert

Rosemaling Inspiration

Linda Goodmon Emery

This original design is based on the rosemaling painting technique. I was inspired to try this technique after seeing a crib quilt made by Helen Kelley. Obtaining the clear, bright colors I wanted to use was a challenge when nearly all fabric was being made in soft, grayed-down colors then. The red fabric, for example, took me a couple of weeks to locate and involved visits to countless quilt shops and fabric stores and probably 400 miles of driving.

81" x 95", Derby, KS, 1986; cottons & flexible ribbon floss embellishment; hand appliqued & hand quilted; Second Place Award, Applique, Professional – 1986 AQS Show.

Roses By Starlight

Although I enjoy all aspects of the quilt-making process, the designing is what I find most stimulating and challenging. "Roses By Starlight" was begun under unusual circumstances. A woman friend was sitting in front of me during a group meeting, and her dress caught my attention – great quilt possibilities! Later I told her I'd buy the dress from her when she was finished with it. She replied, "Oh, I made it and you can have the scraps." The "scraps" turned out to be generous-sized pieces of the blue striped fabric with roses that became the basis for choosing the other fabrics.

89" x 100½", Rochester, NY, 1985; cottons; machine pieced, hand quilted.

Arleen Boyd

Roses For A June Bride

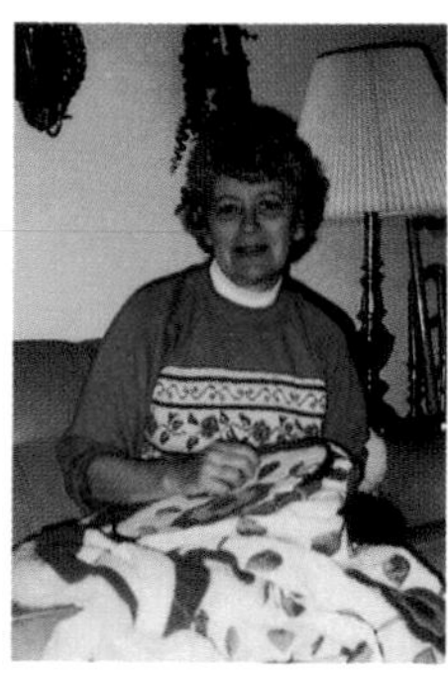

Barbara Brunner

When our daughters were young, I sewed for them, but as they became older, I turned to quilting and lost interest in other crafts. Quilting has given me a way to express my feelings and ideas in my handwork. I love flowers, especially roses and tulips. I do not have an actual flower garden myself, so all my flowers are found on my quilts. I have been quilting for fifteen years and try to quilt every day.

84" x 109", Schofield, WI, 1986; cottons; hand appliqued & hand quilted.

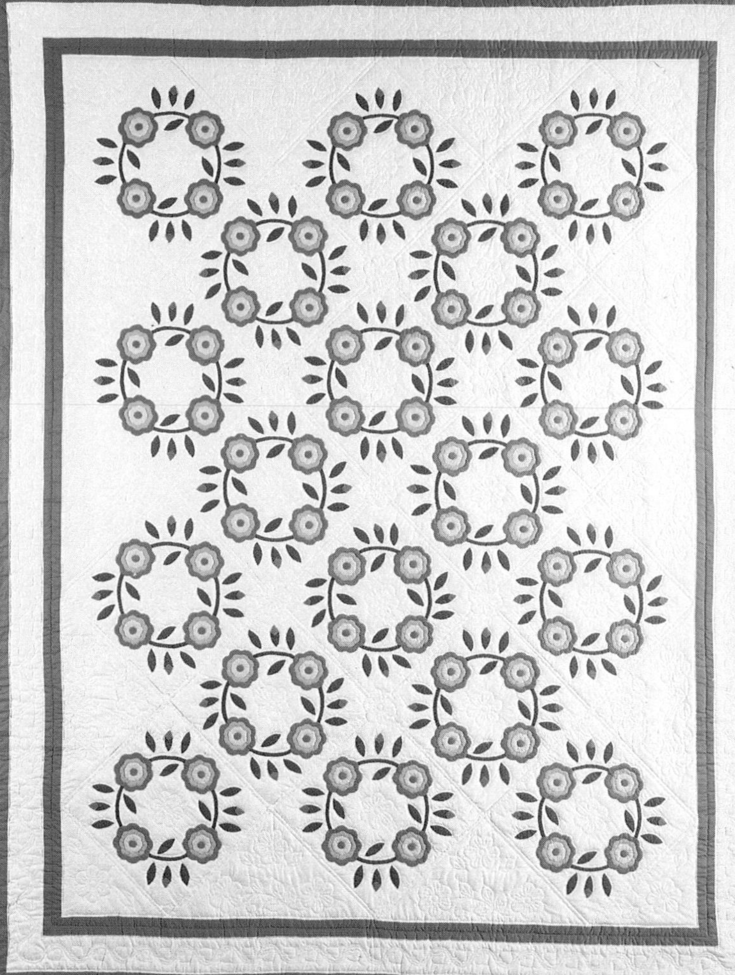

Saturn's Rings

Usually my quilts are original designs or variations of traditional patterns or blocks, but this 1924 Art Deco design just "screamed" at me to be adapted and made into a quilt. "Saturn's Rings" was not made by using an enlarged design as a pattern. Instead, I tore apart my kitchen looking for different size dishes and lids from my pots and pans to use as patterns for the circles. The title was inspired by all the pictures on TV of Saturn and its rings sent back by the space probe.

Quilting is a creative outlet and hobby that brings me joy and happiness. I view the world and life as a series of quilt patterns and I like what I see.

41" x 61", Bay Village, OH, 1986; cottons & linen; hand pieced, hand appliqued & hand quilted.

Susan Knight

Serenity II: Life In My Pond

Donna Duchesne Garofalo

My work is basically representational in style, although some ideas lean more towards the abstract. I enjoy adding fine details that are not immediately noticeable, therefore allowing viewers to make little "discoveries." These details often include embroidery, applique, hand-dyed fabrics, fabric paints and/or quilting designs and fabric patterns that relate in a special way to the subject matter. My love and respect for God's creation and its beauty play an important part in my designing. I consider my abilities a gift from Him.

42" x 57", Chaplin, CT, 1985; cottons & cotton blends; machine pieced, hand appliqued & hand quilted.

Shadow Baltimore Bride

To make this quilt I cut flowers and leaves and laid these pieces on an off-white background with a layer of voile over them. Then, using strands of embroidery floss in a brighter color, I quilted the pieces in between the two layers. When all sections were finished, I sewed them together, added borders, and quilted it again. This is an alternative to an appliqued quilt but looks like applique for those who haven't mastered the art of applique. I feel I can get more detailed with this method than I can with applique. I have done several more quilts using this method and gotten more detailed and intricate in my designs.

86" x 102", Scottdale, PA, 1985; cotton broadcloth, voile & cotton embroidery floss; hand quilted; Third Place Award, Other Techniques, Professional – 1986 AQS Show.

Marian Shenk

Splendor Of The Rajahs

Joyce Stewart

Over the years I had made a few quilts by sewing squares together or just tying two pieces of material together, but I had never made a "real" quilt until the fall of 1981 when I was asked to piece a quilt for our church group. Now I consider myself a true "quilt addict." I think the thing I enjoy most of all in quilting is working with colors. Making the colors work is both challenging and exciting. However, I enjoy the planning, piecing, and quilting and the association with other quilters very much. My "Splendor of the Rajahs" quilt was made using a pattern from the book *Curves Unlimited* by Joyce M. Schlotzhauer.

84" x 106", Rexburg, ID, 1985; cottons; machine pieced & hand quilted.

Spring Flower Basket

*I*n my everyday life I am very much a conformist; however, quilting seems to be my way of breaking the rules and expressing my individuality. I quilt with both hands on top of the quilt, one stitch at a time, make my own thimbles, do not use a quilting needle, use my quilting hoop backward and prefer to work with my own ideas and designs. Prairie points have always held a particular fascination for me because they add texture and dimension to the quilt. I began experimenting with the idea of using them to form the quilt design, resulting in several wallhangings and quilt patterns. Prairie points have now become somewhat of a trademark of my work.

88" x 103", Virginia Beach, VA, 1989; cottons; machine pieced, hand appliqued & hand quilted; Gingher Workmanship Award – 1989 AQS Show.

Janice R. Streeter

Spring Winds

Faye Anderson

"Spring Winds" gave me an opportunity to use a different palette and play with my collection of calico prints. What makes this quilt eye-catching is the fact that applique has been done on a print rather than solid background. I was fortunate to find positive/negative gray and white floral prints that were bold enough to be seen but subdued enough to look neutral behind the darker applique motifs. Since making this quilt I have consciously tried to use prints rather than solids, because it is pattern that most obviously distinguishes works in fabric from those in other mediums, such as paint.

76" x 87", Denver, CO, ©1985; cottons; appliqued; Best of Show Award – 1986 AQS Show.

Springtime Sampler

"Springtime Sampler" is a sampler quilt which incorporates blocks relating to springtime and family memories. The Washington Monument is typical of my geographic area, Washington, D.C. Family pictures are incorporated in the Crazy Patch block. The Courthouse Steps block included symbolizes my lawyer husband. Many of the other blocks used were just fun to do and I made them while teaching machine quiltmaking sampler classes. I have found that I am a much better teacher if I, too, am working on a quilt along with the students.

108" x 108", Rockville, MD, ©1986; cottons; machine pieced & machine quilted; Third Place Award, Traditional Pieced, Professional – 1986 AQS Show.

Lois Smith

Stained Glass Windows

Nadene Zowada

My husband and I lived for 30 years high in the Big Horn Mountains. The long winters provided many hours for all my crafts. I enjoy many types of crafts, creative stitchery, sewing, as well as my quilting projects. "Stained Glass Windows" is a one-of-a-kind quilt. I collected Ed Sibbet books on stained glass projects. Most of the designs were very small so I had to enlarge them to fit a 11" x 14" block. I love the bright earthtone colors. The brown strips were chosen to appear as a wooden wall, thus making the windows even brighter.

98" x 112", Buffalo, WY, 1983; cotton-polyester blends; hand applique.

Star Bright

Quiltmaking is not a part of my heritage. In 1978 I discovered the wonderful world of quilting – via classes, guilds, publications, shows, workshops and contests. It has been a most interesting and fulfilling hobby for me. Because we have no children, I decided I would strive for quality rather than quantity, so each project is a challenge to do my best. I prefer piecework over applique or design. I piece and quilt by hand because the results please me more than my machine work. "Star Bright" was made to enter the Mountain Mist Contest of 1985 and was displayed as one of the finalists.

81" x 96", Livingston, MT, 1985; cottons; hand pieced & hand quilted.

Dorothy Mackley Stovall

STAR-CROSSED

Libby Lehman

"Star-Crossed" is a tribute to my birthplace. Texas is the Lone Star State, known for its wide-open spaces, so the star theme was a natural. The center star radiates out over the rest of the quilt. The background represents the water of the Gulf Coast, a favorite recreation spot of our family. We often sit on the deck of our beach house in the small fishing village of Port O'Connor, located on the Matagorda Bay, and watch the stars as they debut across the night sky. Their reflection on the constantly moving bay waters is depicted in "Star-Crossed.

70" x 70", Houston, TX, 1986; cottons & cotton blends; machine pieced & hand quilted.

STARRY, STARRY NIGHT

Over the years, I feel my approach to quilting has changed considerably. As a member of the Mississippi Valley Quilters Association, I have had the advantage of hearing lectures by nationally known quilters. I have grown to enjoy the challenge of creating quilts unique in both color and design. My philosophy in quilting and in life is the same – you'll never know if you can do it unless you try. "Starry, Starry Night" began with seven yards of horizontal multi-striped fabric. The exterior border corners had to be redesigned due to a shortage of the striped material.

75" x 90", Davenport, IA, 1985; cottons; hand pieced & hand quilted.

Mary Jo McCabe

Strawberry Sundae

Laverne N. Mathews

I started down the quilt primrose path in 1971, and have been totally possessed ever since, making over a hundred myself, collecting old ones, visiting museums where quilts may be seen, taking thousands of pictures, belonging to local, state and national quilt organizations. I served as historian for the Texas Heritage Quilt Society as we documented the old quilts across the entire state of Texas. Making a Strawberry quilt simmered in my mind for a year or two after seeing an antique quilt in the French Trading Post Museum in Beaumont, Texas, the colors so faded you could only imagine what they'd once been.

70" x 84", Orange, TX, 1986; cottons & cotton blends; hand appliqued & hand quilted; Second Place Award, Applique, Amateur – 1987 AQS Show.

Sunset Kites

I started quilting in the 1960's when I had three small children, an Air Force career pilot husband, lots of scraps from small pairs of pajamas and playclothes and a few spare moments. My first quilting frame cost $12.95 from Sears and quilting thread had to be ordered from Stiles Waxt Thread of Sycamore, Illinois – it was a very fine thread that never frayed or tangled. I have made about 65 quilts in 25 years – most of them bed size. I have sold a few but would rather give them to people that I love. I almost always start a new quilt on New Year's Day.

63" x 63", Hillsboro, OR, 1985; cottons; machine pieced & hand quilted.

Carol Ann Wadley

Taos Tapestry

Laverne N. Mathews

I realize in looking back that all my creative endeavors have revolved around COLOR. Mosaics, stained glass, fashions, hooked rugs, and finally – the most rewarding of all – quilting, have as their central essence, glorious color. Color paired with the sensuous quality of fabrics exerts an irresistible tug on the thousands of us who enjoy making quilt art. In addition to colors and textural qualities, quilts have an added appeal – they serve a functional purpose as well!

37" x 40", Orange, TX, 1986; cottons and cotton blends; machine pieced & hand quilted.

TERRARIUM

"Terrarium" was the third in a series of quilts that was inspired by Russian folk art, particularly in its border designs. The terrarium itself superimposes applique on the background fabric that inspired it. I've always been intrigued by the patterns made by shadows against my backyard fences. Always interested in natural cycles, this quilt shows both day and dusk at once and it reflects one of my favorite themes – flowers.

40" x 50½", Evanston, IL, 1983; cottons (some hand dyed); hand appliqued, machine pieced with embroidery & some beadwork.

Marion Huyck

Three For The Crown

Charlotte Warr Andersen

I could have made just a Kentucky Derby Quilt, but when the Derby is finished, one looks to the next big race – the Preakness – and then if the winning horse wins that, on to Belmont and the Belmont Stakes. If the same horse wins that, we have a horse that has become part of a very elite group – the Triple Crown Winners. I love horses and watching horse races – I've been drawing horses since I was a small child, influenced by my father who is a saddlemaker – and I enjoy making quilts that are about American traditions. "Three for the Crown" honors a tradition that is a century strong and one that I hope will be with us for centuries more.

53" x 53", Kearns, UT, 1987; silks; hand pieced (except for the jockeys' hands) & hand quilted; First Place Award, Wall Quilt, Professional – 1987 AQS Show.

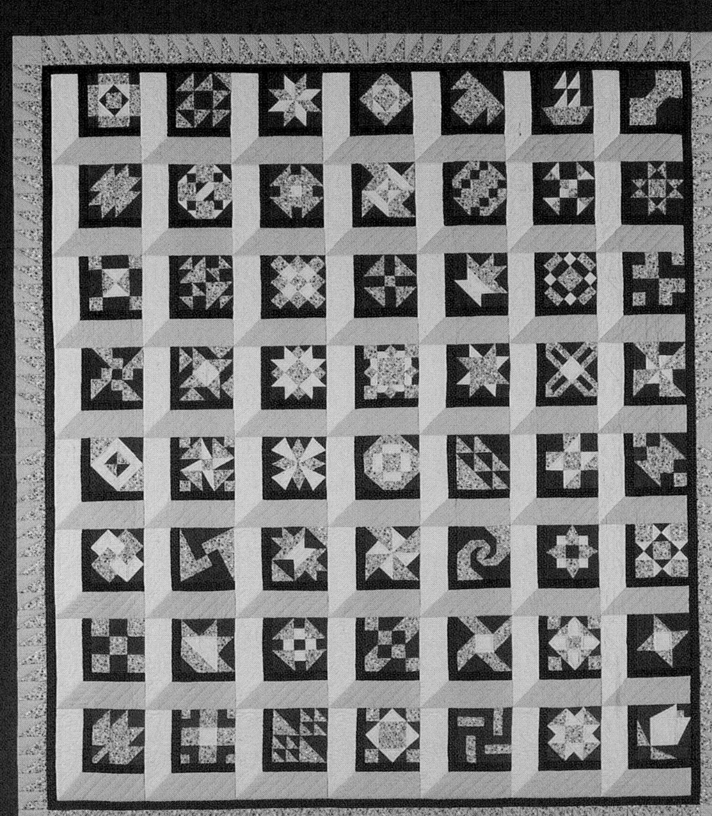

Tradition In The Attic

Margaret Rudd, treasurer of the Trigg County Quilter's Guild, says, "Four of us who are members of the Trigg County Quilter's Guild were enroute home from the 1986 American Quilter's Society Show when one suggested that the guild make a quilt for the next AQS Quilt Show. The suggestion was treated as a joke at first. As the discussion progressed, the challenge was evident...why not? During the months of construction the quilt became known as "the show quilt" and the "for-keeps quilt." Thirty-five individuals worked between 1,200 and 1,300 hours piecing the quilt."

86½" x 94¼", Cadiz, KY, 1988; cottons; hand pieced & hand quilted. On permanent loan from the Trigg County Quilter's Guild.

Trigg County Quilter's Guild

TRANQUILITY

Lillian J. Leonard

I made my first quilt top, a Dresden Plate design, at the age of 11, but quilting was not to become a ruling factor in my life until many years later. A local department store and local newspaper in Indianapolis began co-sponsoring quilt contests about 10 years ago. I entered each of their contests, which were held every two years. I was never among the winners until in 1985 when I designed and entered this quilt, which received an honorable mention. I dream of quilts and quilting patterns – oh for the time to carry out these visions.

78" x 92", Indianapolis, IN, 1985; cottons; hand pieced, hand appliqued & hand quilted.

Trip Around The World

This quilt top containing 2,703 two-inch squares was machine pieced by Mary Carol Goble in Nephi, Utah, and hand quilted by her mother, Verla Hale Adams, in Oakley, Idaho in 1985. Mary Carol has always been fascinated with quilts. Her first was a Nine-Patch she made for her doll when a little girl. Mary Carol has been making all types of quilts for some years. She comments, "Quiltmaking is fascinating to me because I am continually learning something new about it." Verla says that for the past two years, her daughter Mary Carol "has furnished (her) with beautiful pieced quilt tops," for which she has completed the quilting and binding.

105" x 108", Nephi, Utah, 1985; cottons & cotton blends; machine pieced & hand quilted.

Mary Carol Goble & Verla Hale Adams

Tulips Aglow

Mary Kay Hitchner

Quilts are a serious hobby for me. As a non-professional, my goal is to devote more of my time to quiltmaking. Two events led to the creation of this quilt: first, was the purchase of a wonderful floral repeat-stripe fabric that I thought would be a good challenge for me as it was printed in a color palette that I disliked – orange, olive green and khaki; second, was the book review I gave on Marsha McCloskey's *The Feathered Star* for my quilt guild. As a visual aid I made a Feathered Star block which became the central design element for this medallion quilt. I selected the repeat-stripe tulip fabric for the star and outside border. The finished size of the quilt was determined by the yardage I had.

54½" x 54½", Haverford, PA, 1989; cottons; machine pieced & hand quilted; Best Wall Quilt Award – 1990 AQS Show.

Tulips In A Basket

Reared in Trousdale and Macon Counties, Tennessee, where quilting was a family tradition, I learned the fundamentals of quilting at an early age, but didn't begin quilting as an art until the early eighties. "Tulips in a Basket" features 14" blocks adapted from a pattern in the Better Homes and Gardens *Treasury of Needlecrafts*. The design for the quilting was arrived at by use of portions of several quilting patterns from various sources. Portions of the pieced basket and appliqued tulips are stuffed or trapuntoed, to accent the design. As a further accent, trapunto is used around each block, in a ½" wide channel.

87" x 104", Parsons, TN, 1985; cottons; hand appliqued & hand quilted.

Marjorie D. Townsend

Twelve Days Of Christmas

B. J. Elvgren

Inspiration for "Twelve Days of Christmas" was the traditional song along with the self-appointed challenge of using a design to contain the twelve groups within one scene. The Madonna and Christ-child were added as a comment on the foundation of gift-giving at Christmas. The quilt took four months to complete. My ambition continues to be to create art that is enriched by a strong folk heritage and that is a celebration of the wholeness of God's creation.

102" x 108", Pittsburgh, PA, 1983; cottons, velvets & silks; hand appliqued & hand quilted with trapunto & embroidery; First Place Award, Applique, Professional – 1985 AQS Show.

Up, Up & Away

I learned quilting at an early age from my mother, but "Up, Up & Away" was my first original effort. The stuffing technique is my own, and since making this quilt I have continued to perfect it. The design evolved, restricted by the materials I had on hand. The overall concept was inspired by an Oriental rug I saw in a book. I worked for forty years in interior design, and have been teaching design for twenty years in vocational school. My quilting is influenced by my design training.

79" x 79", Cape Girardeau, MO, 1984; cotton chintz; appliqued, stuffed, Seminole piecing.

Laura Crews-Lewis

Victorian Fantasy of Feathers and Lace

Beverly Mannisto Williams

I was unhappy with the disposable, fast-paced state of living and needed something to sink my teeth into. Between part-time work outside the home I took quilt lessons and became hooked. When I learned about the history of bobbin lace, I felt an obligation to pursue that age-old craft too. This quilt was made to let my family know I am very serious about what they consider to be mother's little hobbies. I made the 2½" wide lace from a Finnish design called Milk Pail with bobbins made by my Finnish father, John Mannisto. This quilt was Awarded Masterpiece Quilt Status by the National Quilting Association.

89" x 104", Cadillac, MI, 1986; cotton unbleached muslin & handmade bobbin lace edging; hand quilted; Gingher Workmanship Award – 1987 AQS Show.

Voice Of Freedom

Based on the Lincoln Memorial, this quilt was designed for entry in the Statue of Liberty contest. Unfortunately, it was not completed in time for that contest – it was extremely difficult for me to find commercially dyed fabrics in the exact colors needed to effectively shade the figure. All of the fabrics used were purchased – none were hand-dyed specially for the project. A range of browns and grays were used for the statue and yellow in different values was used in the background to give the effect of the sun shining through.

66" x 65", Marietta, GA, 1987; cottons; hand appliqued & hand quilted.

Barbara Temple

Zinnias In The Windows Of My Log Cabin

Hallie H. O'Kelley

Though I had sewed since girlhood, making many of my family's clothes, I did not make a quilt until 1980. That first quilt was an experiment in using screen printing as a technique for applying the design. Hand quilting was done around the printed design, with the result looking like applique. Since then the idea has been refined. In "Zinnias in the Windows of My Log Cabin," the zinnias were screen printed and the green logs were hand-dyed fabrics.

77" x 85", Tuscaloosa, AL, 1987; cottons; machine pieced & hand quilted; Second Place Award, Theme (Log Cabin) – 1987 AQS Show.

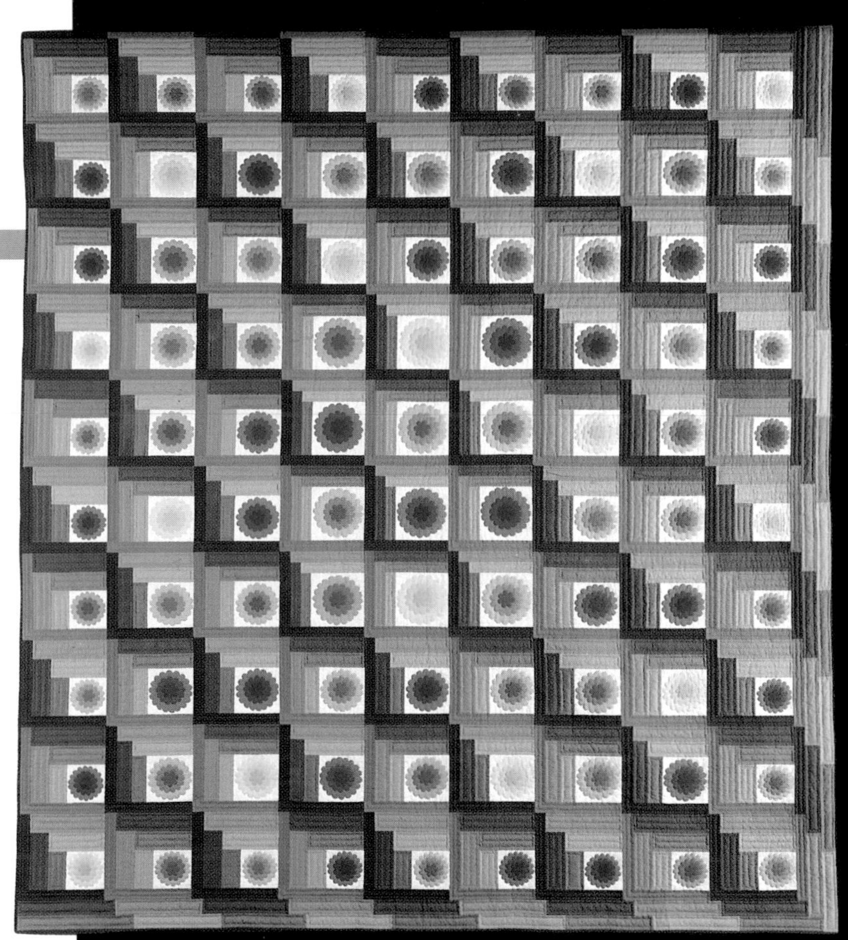

Quiltmakers

Quilts